THERE IS NOBODY *A Direct Pointing to Truth*

First Edition: 2025

ISBN:

AF657933

Published by: [Self-published / Manoj Ashok Kandhari]

Cover design: [Joshita/Srushti)

Disclaimer: This book reflects the author's personal spiritual insights and philosophical reflections. It is intended to inspire contemplation rather than prescribe belief or practice. The experiences described are individual and subjective, not universal truths.

This work is not a substitute for medical, psychological, or spiritual counseling. Readers are encouraged to exercise personal discernment and seek professional guidance where appropriate.

The author and publisher accept no responsibility for how the content is interpreted or applied.

Neither the author nor the publisher shall be liable for any loss or damage arising directly or indirectly from the use of this material.

Contact: [livingintao@yahoo.com]

Dedicated to My Final Teacher

CONTENTS

PREFACE

This book is for you.

Not for the casually curious. Not for those collecting spiritual knowledge. Not for those seeking to build a more refined version of themselves.

But for you - the one who has exhausted seeking. The one who has tried everything and found nothing works—the one standing at the edge, ready for the final step.

You've read the scriptures. Listened to teachers. Done the practices. Had glimpses of truth. Yet something persists - a subtle sense of "not quite there yet," of still being someone who needs to become something.

This book will not give you more knowledge. Will not offer you new practices. Will not promise you future attainment.

This book points directly to what you already are. Not as a philosophy. Not as a belief. But as an invitation to look right now and see what's actually true.

The teaching is simple: There is nobody. There never was. All seeking is based on the fiction that there's someone who needs liberation.

When you look for this "someone" and cannot find them, the search comes to an end. Not because you found what you were seeking, but because the seeker was seen as an illusion.

What remains is not "you enlightened." What remains is just this - life happening, consciousness present, existence unfolding - without anyone at the center claiming it.

This is not comfortable. Not gentle. Not gradual.

This is the final dissolution. The complete seeing-through. The end of postponement.

If you're truly ready—not theoretically ready, but actually exhausted with being someone—then read on. Let the pointing cut through every defense, every strategy, every last hiding place of the seeker.

If you're not ready, if you still crave spiritual experiences, states, or gradual progress, put this book down. Come back when seeking has exhausted itself completely.

But if you're done - truly done - with the game of becoming, then this book is for you!

Not to give you something. But to show you what was never absent.

Not to make you into nobody. But to reveal you never were somebody.

The teaching is offered. The transmission is complete.

The rest is up to nobody.

CHAPTER 1: The Urgency

Why This Cannot Wait

You have read the texts. You recognize the promise: life becomes blissful, joyful, eternal once you seek the truth. The spiritual books speak of liberation, enlightenment, and freedom. Beautiful words. Inspiring concepts.

But let me ask you directly: Are you free?

Right now, reading this - are you free from suffering? Free from anxiety about the future? Free from regret about the past? Free from the nagging sense that something is missing, that you're not quite there yet?

If the answer is no, then all the reading has done nothing. All the knowledge has brought you no closer. You are still bound.

And the binding is not complex. It has one root cause.

Ignorance.

The Root of All Suffering

Not ignorance of spiritual teachings - you may know plenty of those.

Not ignorance of practices - you may have tried many.

But ignorance of what you actually are.

This ignorance is the root that binds you to a belief system. A system that acknowledges truth the way it has been explained to you, taught to you, conditioned into you - but not the way it actually IS.

You believe you are a person. A body-mind living in the world. A someone with a past, a future, problems to solve, goals to achieve. This belief feels so obvious, so self-evident, that you never question it.

And this unquestioned belief is your prison.

What a True Seeker Actually Needs

Not more books. Not more practices. Not more teachers, techniques, or traditions.

A true seeker needs only three things:

1. Earnestness to be free

Not casual interest. Not a spiritual hobby. But burning necessity. The kind of urgency a drowning person has for air. The type of commitment that says: "I need truth more than comfort, more than security, more than anything else."

Without this earnestness, nothing moves. You can read a thousand books, attend a hundred retreats, practice for decades - and remain exactly where you are. Because you're not truly seeking freedom. You're seeking better bondage.

2. Maturity to drop what doesn't serve anymore

Even - especially - what is dear to you.

Your beliefs about yourself. Your spiritual identity. Your accumulated knowledge. Your cherished practices. Your relationship with your favorite teachers and teachings.

Can you drop them? Not theoretically. Actually. When the moment comes, when you see they are obstacles rather than aids, can you let them go?

Most cannot. They've invested too much and built too much identity around being spiritual seekers. The thought of dropping it all feels like death.

It is death. Death of the false. And that death is absolutely necessary.

3. Authenticity to allow being exposed

So that all that is not you surfaces and leaves.

This means being willing to see your own self-deception. Your spiritual bypassing. Your subtle seeking of experiences and states. Your investment in remaining someone who is becoming enlightened rather than recognizing you are already what you seek.

It means being willing to be seen - by a teacher, by truth itself - in all your strategies, all your resistance, all your clinging.

Most people want truth, but only if they can keep their comfortable illusions intact. They want freedom, but don't want to be exposed. They want liberation, but on their own terms.

It doesn't work that way.

When the Path Becomes Clear

When these three are present - earnestness, maturity, authenticity - the path becomes clear.

Not because you've learned something new.

But because all the obstacles you were carrying have been dropped.

And here's the remarkable thing: **It is only when the real search begins.**

Everything before that - all the years of reading, practicing, seeking - was preparation at best, postponement at worst.

The real search begins when you stop looking for better experiences, deeper states, more knowledge, and future attainment—and start looking directly at who is seeking all of this.

Who are you?

Not philosophically. Not conceptually. But actually - right now - who are you?

Can you find yourself? Can you point to the one reading these words? Can you prove this "you" exists as anything other than a thought, a belief, an assumption?

This is the real search. And it can happen now. Not after more preparation. Not after completing some system or practice. Now.

The Long Route vs. The Direct Path

In the Yoga Sutras of Patanjali, the great sage discusses the eight limbs of yoga. Yama, niyama, asana, pranayama, pratyahara, dharana, dhyana, samadhi. A complete system, carefully structured, progressively refined.

And after discussing all eight limbs, after laying out this comprehensive path, Patanjali finally tells you: Now is the time to go inward.

Now. After all that. The time to actually look.

Not many people complete even half of these limbs in their lifetime. Though they think they do. They practice asana for years, work on pranayama, and attempt concentration. All valuable. All is useful as preparation.

But why use such a long route when there is a direct path?

Sri Ramana Maharshi suggested this in all his talks, as recorded in *Self-Realization: The Life and Teachings of Ramana Maharshi.* The direct path of self-enquiry. Not after you've perfected your body through asana, or your breath through pranayama, or your mind through meditation.

But now. Right now. Whoever you are, whatever condition you're in, whatever level of practice you've achieved or not achieved.

Ask: "Who am I?"

And look. Directly. Immediately.

It is possible, right here and now.

Not as a theory. Not as hope for the future. But as actual recognition that can happen in this moment.

The question is not whether it's possible.

The question is: **Are you ready?**

The Choice Before You

You can postpone this. Tell yourself you need more preparation, more practice, more knowledge, that you're not ready yet. That someday, when conditions are right, when you've completed your practices, when you've found the perfect teacher - then you'll look directly.

This postponement can last several lifetimes.

Or you can look now.

Not after finishing this book. Not after one more retreat. Not after resolving your life circumstances.

But now. This moment. As you read these words.

Who is reading? Can you find them? Where are they? What are they made of?

Look and see.

Because the truth is: you're not going to become more ready. You won't reach a point where it's easier. You're not going to find a better moment.

This moment is it.

The only moment there is. The only moment there ever was. The only moment in which truth can be recognized.

Not in some imagined future.

But here.

Now.

Are you willing to look?

Or will you close this book, add it to your collection of spiritual texts, and continue postponing what has already been postponed for lifetimes?

The choice is yours.

But know this: the suffering will continue as long as the ignorance continues. The seeking will continue as long as the seeker remains unquestioned. The postponement will continue as long as you believe "later" is an option.

There is no later.

There is only now.

And in this now, the question stands:

Who are you?

Look.

CHAPTER 2: Recognition Vs. Glimpse

Why Experiences Don't Last

You've had it before - that moment of clarity.

Perhaps during meditation, or in nature, or in a moment of crisis. Suddenly, the boundaries dissolve. The separation between "you" and "everything else" vanishes. There's just this - vast, open, undivided presence.

For seconds, minutes, maybe hours, you know beyond doubt: *This is it. This is what all the teachings point to.*

And then it fades.

The person returns. The world becomes solid again. The separation re-establishes itself. And you're left with a memory of something extraordinary that happened to someone - the someone you think you are.

This is a glimpse. And it is not liberation.

The Seeker's Most Dangerous Trap

Glimpses are beautiful. They show you what's possible. They confirm that the teachings aren't just philosophy - there really is something beyond the ordinary experience of being a separate person.

But glimpses are also the seeker's most dangerous trap.

Because after a glimpse, the seeker has something to seek. "I've tasted it. Now I need to get back there. I need to make it permanent. I need to become the person who lives in that state all the time."

The seeker becomes more convinced than ever that they exist - because after all, they had an awakening experience. They tasted enlightenment. They are someone special now, someone on the path, someone who knows.

And this is precisely the problem.

The glimpse happened TO someone. Recognition reveals there is no one for anything to happen to.

What Actually Happened

An illustration: During a meditation retreat, after years of practice, I reached complete exhaustion with seeking. Frustration, sleepiness, failure - the seeker was worn out. In that exhaustion, sitting by a rivulet, I gave up completely. Shouted at the sky: "I give up. Now you chase me."

That afternoon, in the meditation hall, silence descended naturally. Opening my eyes, I saw: I am the tree, the bird, the people sitting here. Everything was me. No separation. The urge to serve arose spontaneously - washing everyone's dishes, knowing I was washing my own.

This was a glimpse. Beautiful. Undeniable in that moment. But still an experience happening to someone. Something I could remember, talk about, claim as "my awakening."

The doubts came afterward. "Was that real? Just an experience? An altered state?" The glimpse faded. The person reformed. And seeking resumed - now seeking to recapture that experience, to make it permanent.

Recognition: The End of the Experiencer

Recognition is entirely different.

Recognition doesn't happen TO someone. It's the seeing-through of the one who would have experiences.

In a glimpse:

- There's an experience of oneness
- Someone experiences it
- It comes and goes
- Memory remains: "I had an awakening"
- Seeking continues: "How do I get back there?"

In recognition:

- There's the seeing that there never was someone
- No one to have the experience
- Nothing to come or go
- No memory of "my enlightenment" because there's no one to claim it
- Seeking ends because the seeker is seen as illusion

The glimpse says: "I am everything."

Recognition says: "There is no 'I' to be anything."

Can you feel the difference?

One still has a subject claiming unity. The other has no subject at all.

Why Glimpses Don't Stabilize

This is why glimpses, no matter how profound, don't lead to stable freedom.

Because the structure remains intact: someone who had an experience and wants more of it.

You might chase that glimpse for years, decades, lifetimes. Meditating more intensely. Going on more retreats. Finding new teachers. Trying different practices. All seeking to recapture what was temporarily experienced.

However, the very act of seeking perpetuates the seeker. The very effort to become enlightened confirms there's someone who isn't enlightened yet.

It's like trying to find yourself by running away from yourself. The faster you run, the more you're still there, running.

The Question That Ends the Seeking

There's only one way out of this trap:

Stop seeking the experience. Start investigating the experiencer.

Not "How do I get back to that state of oneness?"

But "Who is trying to get back? Who had the experience? Who wants enlightenment?"

Look for that one. Can you find them?

When you look directly - not think about it, but actually look - what do you find?

Thoughts appear: "I am this body." "I am this mind." "I am the one seeking."

But these are just thoughts. Can you find the actual "I" they refer to? Can you locate it? Point to it? Prove it exists as anything other than an assumption?

This is not philosophy. This is direct investigation.

Look now. Right now. Who is reading these words?

From Experience to Being

The glimpse is a gift. It shows you what's possible. It breaks the certainty that you're just a body-mind in the world.

But don't make it a prison. Don't spend the rest of your life chasing the repetition of an experience.

Instead, use the glimpse as a pointer:

If in that moment there was no separation, no solid "me" - then what created the separation before and after? What made "me" seem real?

Investigation. Not experience.

The glimpse says: "See what's possible."

Recognition says: "See what's always been true."

The glimpse is temporary.

Recognition is not a state that comes and goes. It's seeing that what you are never changes, never moves, never experiences anything - because experiences happen IN it, not TO it.

The Shift From Seeking States to Seeing Truth

As long as you're seeking enlightenment as a better experience, a higher state, a permanent bliss - you're still the person seeking improvement.

The person can never be enlightened. The person IS the problem.

So the question shifts:

From: "How do I achieve/maintain/stabilize that experience?"

To: "Who is seeking? Can I find them?"

And when you cannot find the seeker - what remains?

Not as an experience. Not as a state. Not as something that came.

But as the simple, obvious fact that was always here.

That tree outside the window, that bird chirping, these words being read - they're not appearing to someone. They're appearing in awareness. AS awareness. Without a separate experiencer making claims about them.

This is not a glimpse to achieve.

This is the ground you've never left.

The question is: Are you willing to stop seeking experiences and look directly at who's seeking?

Because in that looking, the glimpse becomes irrelevant.

And what remains needs no repetition, no maintenance, no practice to sustain it.

It is simply what is.

Always has been.

Always will be.

Look.

CHAPTER 3: When Death Tests Your Understanding

The Difference Between Knowing and Being

You can know intellectually that you are not the body. You can repeat the teaching: "I am not this body-mind, I am pure awareness."

You can have glimpses where this feels true. Moments of meditation where identification with the body loosens, where you experience yourself as spacious awareness rather than limited form.

But then the body gets sick. Or faces death. And in that moment, you discover whether your understanding is real or merely conceptual.

Because when death becomes actual - not philosophical, not something happening to others, but knocking at your own door - everything false falls away. Only what's real remains.

The Ultimate Test

Spiritual understanding that cannot face death is still just a thought. Still just a belief. Still, the person holding ideas about non-duality while secretly believing they are the body.

Death is the ultimate test of recognition.

Not because you need to prove anything. But because death strips away all pretense. All spiritual positions. All comfortable beliefs.

When you're told your body may die - truly may die, not someday in the distant future but soon - one of two things happens:

Either terror arises (revealing that, despite all your understanding, you still believe you ARE this body)

Or peace remains (revealing that recognition has gone deeper than thought, deeper than belief, into actual knowing).

An Illustration From Crisis

Six months after that glimpse by the rivulet, diagnosis came: aortic aneurysm. A weakness in the heart's main vessel. Could rupture anytime—death, sudden and final.

The months between diagnosis and surgery were a different kind of spiritual practice. Not meditation on cushions. But facing mortality directly. Watching the mind's terror arise. Watching hope and despair alternate. Watching the person who thought they "understood" non-duality face the prospect of this body ending.

All the spiritual seeking intensified paradoxically. More practices, more desperation. "If I'm going to die, I need to wake up BEFORE that happens." As if enlightenment were an achievement to collect before time runs out.

But underneath the seeking, something else held. That recognition - that I am not this body - wasn't completely gone. It was there, like a note held beneath all the noise.

August came. Surgery scheduled. Open-heart surgery. Hours when this body might not wake up.

The night before, a clarity arose. Not forced, not practiced. Just simple seeing: What is there to fear? What can be lost that's actually mine?

The morning of surgery, on the operating table, just before anesthesia - a moment of total surrender. Not to death. Not to survival. But to truth itself.

The wish that arose was this: "Let this life continue if moksha is possible. If not, let it go with this surgery."

Not "please save me." Not "I want to live." But complete willingness for the body to end if liberation wasn't possible through it.

The person couldn't have made that wish. Only recognition could. Only the knowing that what I am doesn't die with the body.

The body survived. The heart was repaired. But something else shifted in that moment of total acceptance. The recognition that had been glimpsed moved deeper. Not into a permanent state. But into lived knowing.

What Death Reveals

The greatest example of death as investigation comes from Ramana Maharshi himself, as recorded in *Self-Realization: The Life and Teachings of Ramana Maharshi.*

At sixteen years old, without any prior spiritual practice, Ramana was suddenly gripped by an intense fear of death. The body became stiff, as if death were actually happening. But instead of panicking, instead of running to find help, something prompted him to investigate.

He lay down. Made the body stiff like a corpse. And asked: "What is this death?"

The body dies - he could see that clearly. It would become a corpse, be carried to the cremation ground, and burned to ashes.

But "I" - what happens to "I"?

In that moment of facing death directly, of investigating while the fear of death gripped the body, recognition happened.

The body may die. But "I" - awareness itself, consciousness itself, the Self - does not die. Cannot die. Was never born to die.

This was not philosophy. Not belief. Not hope for immortality. But direct seeing: the "I" that he had always taken to be the body was actually independent of the body. Prior to the body. Untouched by what happens to the body.

From that moment, Ramana's identification with the body ended completely. He knew beyond doubt: I am not this body. I am that which observes the body, which exists before the body, which continues regardless of what happens to the body.

This investigation, which faced death directly and asked "Who dies?" became the foundation of his teaching. Because death strips away all pretense. All spiritual concepts. All comfortable beliefs. It reveals what's real.

Death - or the real prospect of it - reveals whether your understanding is:

Intellectual: "I know I'm not the body" (but secretly believe I am)

Experiential: "I've had glimpses of being more than body" (but still identify as a person who has experiences)

Actual: "There is no one to die" (the person is already seen as an illusion, death changes nothing fundamental)

Most seekers are at level one or two. They think they're at level three because they can talk about non-duality, quote the masters, and describe awakening experiences.

But when death comes - or serious illness, or loss, or any genuine threat to the body-mind - the truth reveals itself.

If terror arises, if desperate clinging to survival takes over, if the spiritual understanding disappears under the weight of actual fear - then it was still just thought—still just the person's philosophy.

If peace remains - not cold indifference, but simple acceptance that what you are cannot be threatened by what happens to the body - then recognition has stabilized beyond concept.

Ramana showed this perfectly. At sixteen, with no preparation, he faced death and saw through it completely. That seeing never left him. For the remaining fifty-four years of his life, he knew with absolute certainty: I am not this body.

The Body May Suffer, But What Are You?

This doesn't mean the body won't react. Pain will still hurt. Fear may still arise as a biological response. The body-mind has its own survival mechanisms.

But the question is: Who is experiencing this?

Is there someone who IS the body, whose existence depends on the body's survival?

Or is the body appearing in awareness, like everything else, without a separate "you" who owns it or will end when it ends?

Ramana Maharshi's body had cancer. It caused tremendous pain. Devotees asked him, "Bhagavan, doesn't it hurt?"

He replied, as recorded in *Self-Realization*: "There is pain. But I am not in pain."

The body experiences pain. But the Self - what you actually are - is untouched.

This is not philosophy to believe. It's what direct investigation reveals.

From Philosophy to Recognition

So, how does understanding move from intellectual to actual?

Not by thinking harder about it. Not by accumulating more knowledge about non-duality.

But by investigating directly: Who would die?

Right now, before any actual death threat, while you're healthy and comfortable - look.

If this body died tomorrow, what would be lost?

Not the body - obviously that would be lost. Not the memories, the personality, the life story - those would end.

But YOU - can you find this "you" that would be lost?

Look for it. Seriously. Earnestly. Not as an intellectual exercise but as an actual investigation.

Where is this "you" that's reading these words? Can you locate it? Point to it? Find it as something separate from thoughts, sensations, perceptions?

When you look and cannot find it, what remains?

That which remains - that which is looking, that which is aware, that which cannot be found as an object - that doesn't die when the body dies.

Not because it's an immortal soul (that's still a concept). But because it was never born. Never separate. Never a "thing" that could end.

The Practice of Dying Daily

You don't need to wait for an actual death threat to test your understanding.

You can investigate now. Daily.

What if this body died today? Right now? What would actually be lost?

Not what the mind imagines would be lost. But actually - can you find something that would cease to exist?

When you cannot find the one who would die, fear of death loses its grip.

Not because you've convinced yourself of immortality. But because you've seen directly that there's no one to die.

The body will die. That's certain. But were you ever the body? Look and see.

The person will end. That's inevitable. But were you ever a person? Or was "person" just a thought appearing in awareness?

This investigation, done earnestly, done honestly, done without seeking comfort or conclusion - this reveals what death cannot touch.

What Remains When Everything Is Lost

After surgery, after facing death and surviving, what had changed?

Not the circumstances. The body still had to recover. Life still had its challenges. The world was still the world.

But the relationship to all of it had shifted. Not dramatically. Not like the glimpse by the rivulet. But more fundamentally.

The recognition wasn't "I am everything" anymore. It was simpler: "There is no one this is happening to."

Events happen. The body experiences. Emotions arise. But there's no separate owner of these experiences. No person to whom life is happening.

This is what death tests and what survives the test: the simple seeing that there never was anyone to be threatened.

Not as a belief. Not as hope. But as direct, undeniable recognition.

For You, Facing Your Own Mortality

You will die. Not someday in theory, but actually. This body will end. The person you think you are will cease.

This is not morbid. This is liberating.

Because if you investigate now - while alive, while healthy, while the mind isn't clouded by actual crisis - you can discover what doesn't die.

Not by believing in the afterlife or reincarnation. Those are still concepts, still beliefs of the person.

But by seeing directly, there is no person to die in the first place.

The body-mind appears. Functions. Will end.

But what you are - that which is aware of the body-mind, that in which the body-mind appears - that has no beginning or end.

Not because it's eternal. But because it's not a thing. Not an entity. Not something that could be born or could die.

Look now. Don't wait for death to force the investigation.

Who are you that could die? Can you find this one?

When you cannot find them, what remains is what was always here, before birth, beyond death, untouched by the coming and going of bodies, thoughts, worlds.

That is what you are.

Not as philosophy.

As direct seeing.

Look.

CHAPTER 4: Recognizing Your Final Teacher

When the Seeker Meets the End

You've met many teachers. Read many books. Attended many retreats. Each one promising something, pointing somewhere, offering a method or practice or teaching.

Some resonated deeply. Some didn't land at all. Most were genuine in their way, serving exactly what was needed at that moment.

And through it all, the seeking continued. The seeker remained. The sense of "I need to find the right teacher, the right path, the right techniquc" persisted.

This is the spiritual marketplace. And you can spend lifetimes there, collecting teachings like stones, hoping one will finally deliver what all the others promised but didn't provide.

But there comes a moment - if you're fortunate, if grace moves, if earnestness has reached critical mass - when you meet something different.

Not another teacher to add to your collection.

But the one who ends the collecting itself.

What Makes a Final Teacher Different?

A final teacher is not better than other teachers. Not more enlightened, not more powerful, not more charismatic.

A final teacher is simply the one who doesn't give you what you want.

Every other teacher, every other teaching, gave you something to do, something to practice, something to become. They confirmed the seeker. They said: "Yes, you need improvement. Here's how to improve."

The final teacher says: "Stop. There is nothing to do. There is no one to improve. Everything you're seeking is the obstacle."

Papaji expressed this most directly in his Satsang videos: "Don't move. Don't make any effort. Just keep quiet and see what you are."

This is not what the seeker wants to hear.

The seeker wants: "Do this practice, follow this path, and you'll reach enlightenment."

The final teacher says: "There is no path. There is no enlightenment to reach. There is no you to reach it. Stop seeking and see what's already here."

The seeker is devastated. Confused. Angry even.

Because if there's nothing to do, no path to follow, no goal to achieve - then what was all that seeking for? What was the point of all those years of practice?

And that devastation, that confusion, that anger - that's the beginning of the end of seeking.

The Test of Earnestness

A final teacher doesn't accept everyone. Can't accept everyone.

Because the teaching is not about giving information or techniques. It's about dismantling the seeker. And only those who are ready - truly ready - can undergo that dismantling without running away.

The test is simple but ruthless: How earnest are you?

Not "how much do you want enlightenment?" That's still seeking.

But "are you willing to give up being someone who seeks enlightenment?"

Are you willing to drop your spiritual identity? Your accumulated knowledge? Your cherished practices? Your relationship with your favorite teachings?

Are you willing to be nobody?

Most people fail this test. They come to the final teacher, hear the pointing, and run back to the familiar. Back to practices that confirm them as practitioners. Back to teachings that promise future attainment. Back to the comfortable spiritual identity they've built.

Only those who are exhausted - truly exhausted - with seeking stay. Only those who would rather die than continue seeking one more day's stay. Only those who are ready to lose everything stay.

How Recognition Happens

An illustration: After years of practices, teachers, retreats - after glimpses that faded and seeking that intensified - a friend called one Friday morning.

"There's someone who speaks the truth differently. He's been to a master in India. You should meet him."

Why go? I'd met many teachers. What would be different this time?

But something in the friend's voice. Something about "speaks the truth differently." And most of all, the exhaustion. The absolute weariness of collecting one more teaching, one more stone.

That afternoon, in a cafe, the man asked two simple questions:

"What are you looking for? How important is it to you?"

The answer came from somewhere beyond strategy, beyond seeking to impress: "I need the Truth. I am ready to die for it at this moment. Nothing else matters."

This wasn't spiritual talk. It was a confession—an admission of complete desperation.

He spoke for twenty minutes. Not from scriptures, not from concepts. Just pointing to the wholeness and completeness of everything, right now, as it is.

And in that pointing, something recognized: This is it. This is the one who will push me from the cliff.

Not gently guide. Not gradually lead. But push completely. The final dissolution.

The Bigger Hand and the Smaller Hand

My teacher said it perfectly: "A bigger hand is for you to get closer to the truth. A smaller hand is to help you realize it - or rather, to be found by it."

Some teachers are the bigger hand. They hold you, prepare you, bring you closer through devotion, through practice, through gradual refinement. They meet you where you are and work with what you have.

This is necessary. This is grace. Without the bigger hand, most seekers would never develop the capacity for the final teaching.

But at some point, the bigger hand must release you to the smaller hand.

The smaller hand doesn't hold you. Doesn't carry you. Doesn't give you comfort or gradual progress.

The smaller hand points precisely: Look here. See this. There is nothing to become. There is no one becoming it. Stop and recognize what's already apparent.

This pointing is final because it leaves no room for seeking. No path to follow. No practice to do. No future attainment to hope for.

Just: Look now. What are you? Can you find the seeker? When you cannot, what remains?

The Month of Investigation

What follows meeting the final teacher is not bliss. Not instant enlightenment. Not peaceful surrender.

What follows is the systematic dismantling of every defense, every strategy, every subtle way the seeker tries to survive.

This is where maturity really matters.

You cannot feel hurt when your beliefs are shattered. You cannot take it personally when your spiritual identity is exposed as fiction. You cannot resist when everything you thought you knew is shown to be a concept.

Maturity means being ready for the jump. Not holding back. Not protecting yourself. Not saying "yes, but..."

It means complete willingness to be dismantled, exposed, dissolved - without complaint, without defense, without the person trying to save itself.

Without this maturity, you'll run. The pointing will feel too harsh, too direct, too uncompromising. You'll go back to gentler teachings, more gradual paths, teachers who confirm rather than destroy you.

But with maturity, each dismantling is welcomed. Each exposure is liberation. Each death of a false belief is closer to what's real.

Each day, a fresh investigation. Each day, the mind tries new tricks to avoid the final seeing. Each day, those tricks are exposed.

"But I had an awakening" - seen through. "But I understand non-duality" - seen through. "But I'm already awake, I just need to stabilize it" - seen through.

Every claim to knowledge, every spiritual position, every identity - dismantled.

This is not comfortable. Emotions arise - joy at moments of clarity, fear at moments of losing ground. The person fights for survival even as it's being seen through.

But with earnestness, with maturity, with willingness to be exposed completely - something cracks open.

Not a new experience. Not a special state. But the simple seeing: There is nobody. There never was. All the seeking was the phantom seeking itself.

"Don't Tell Me You Already Knew"

The final teacher's words were precise: "Don't ever tell me that you already knew what I pointed you to."

This cuts through the spiritual ego's last defense.

The seeker wants to claim: "Yes, I've always known this. I just forgot. Now I remember."

But no. What's being recognized now is not what was glimpsed before. Glimpses had an experiencer. This has none. Glimpses were experiences. This is not an experience - it's the ground from which all experiences emerge.

The difference between glimpse and recognition, between understanding and being, between knowing about truth and being truth - this is what the final teacher reveals.

And that revelation confirms nothing. Gives nothing. Leaves no one who can claim "I got it."

Only the simple, obvious fact: There is no one. There never was. All seeking was based on a fiction.

How to Recognize Your Final Teacher

You'll know.

Not because they're famous or have many followers. Not because they speak most eloquently or have the most impressive credentials.

But because when you meet them, something in you recognizes: This is the end of seeking.

Not "this is the next step on my path."

But "this is where the path ends. This is where the seeker dies."

That recognition may come with fear. With resistance. With the person's desperate attempt to maintain itself.

But if you're truly earnest, if you're truly exhausted, if you're truly ready - you stay.

You stay through the dismantling. Through the exposure. Through the death of everything you thought you were and everything you hoped to become.

And what remains after that death is not achievement. Not attainment. Not enlightenment that "you" finally reached.

But the simple recognition that there was never anyone to reach anything. That what you are was always already complete, always already free, always already home.

The final teacher doesn't give you this. The final teacher simply points to what was always obvious but overlooked in all the seeking.

And when the seeking ends - not because you got what you sought, but because the seeker is seen as illusion - only truth remains.

Not as something gained.

But as what was never lost.

For You, Still Seeking

Are you ready to meet your final teacher?

Not "ready" as in sufficiently prepared, sufficiently practiced, sufficiently spiritual.

But ready as in: willing to give up seeking. Willing to die as the seeker. Willing to lose your spiritual identity, your accumulated knowledge, your cherished path.

If yes - truly yes, not "maybe someday" - then you're ready.

The teacher will appear. Or you'll recognize what's already here, which is the same thing.

But if you're still shopping, still collecting teachings, still hoping to add one more technique or practice or insight to your repertoire - then you're not ready.

And that's fine. Keep seeking until seeking exhausts itself. Keep collecting stones until you realize they're all stones.

Just know: the final teacher is not another stone to collect.

The final teacher is the one who shows you there's no one collecting anything.

And in that showing, the search ends.

Not because you found what you were seeking.

But because the seeker was seen as fiction.

And what remains needs no teacher, no teaching, no path, no practice.

It simply is.

Always was.

Always will be.

Look.

CHAPTER 5: Earnestness

The Non-Negotiable Requirement

You can have the perfect teacher. The clearest pointing. The most direct method.

And none of it will matter if you lack one thing: earnestness.

Not sincerity. Not interest. Not even dedication.

But earnestness - the burning, desperate need for truth that makes everything else secondary.

Without this, spiritual seeking becomes a hobby. Philosophy. Identity building. Entertainment.

With this, liberation is inevitable.

Not because you earn it through earnestness. But because earnestness is the dissolution of everything that obscures what you already are.

What Earnestness Actually Is

Earnestness is not something you do. Not a quality you cultivate. Not a practice you perform.

Earnestness is the recognition that nothing else matters.

Not "I want enlightenment and also a good career and loving relationships and..."

But "I need truth. Period. Everything else is negotiable."

Ramana spoke of the drowning man's desire for air, as recorded in *Self-Realization*. When your head is held underwater, you don't casually wish for breath. You don't intellectually understand that oxygen would be nice. You need air with your entire being. Every cell screams for it. Nothing else exists in that moment except the desperate need to breathe.

Nisargadatta Maharaj made earnestness the absolute requirement. In *I Am That*, he repeatedly emphasized: "Earnestness is the most important thing. If you are earnest, you have already succeeded. Everything else will follow." He turned away those who came with casual curiosity, who wanted to debate philosophy, who sought experiences. But those who came with burning need - desperate, exhausted, ready to give everything - he worked with relentlessly until recognition happened.

That intensity. That single-pointed necessity. That complete subordination of everything to one thing.

That's earnestness.

The Test of Earnestness

When the final teacher asks: "How important is this to you?" - it's not a rhetorical question.

It's a test.

Because your answer reveals everything.

If you say: "Very important. One of my top priorities. I meditate daily and attend retreats..."

The teacher knows: You're not ready. You're collecting spiritual experiences, building spiritual identity, hoping to improve yourself. But you're not desperate for truth.

If you say: "I need the Truth. I am ready to die for it at this moment. Nothing else matters."

And you mean it - not as performance, not as what you think you should say, but as confession of actual fact - then the teacher knows: You're ready. Earnestness is present. The dismantling can begin.

The test is not about right words. It's about the reality behind the words.

Are you willing to give up everything? Your comfort, your relationships, your security, your identity, your beliefs, your accumulated spiritual knowledge - everything?

Not theoretically. Actually. If truth required it, would you give it all up right now?

If the answer is yes without hesitation, earnestness is present.

If there's even a moment of "well, but I need to..." - then seeking continues, but earnestness hasn't ripened yet.

Can Earnestness Be Cultivated?

This is the paradox.

Earnestness cannot be manufactured. You cannot force yourself to be more earnest. Cannot practice earnestness. Cannot will yourself into desperate need for truth.

Yet earnestness does develop. Does ripen. Does emerge through the process of seeking itself.

How?

Through exhaustion.

You seek pleasure - get it - find it doesn't satisfy. You seek success - achieve it - find it doesn't complete you. You seek relationships - have them - find they don't fill the emptiness. You seek spiritual experiences - have them - find they fade.

Each disappointment, each recognition that "this isn't it," each exhaustion of another avenue of seeking - this builds earnestness.

Not by becoming more desperate for what you haven't found.

But by becoming exhausted with seeking itself.

Until finally, you're not seeking better experiences, deeper states, higher consciousness.

You're seeking only truth. Only what's real. Only what doesn't come and go.

This is when earnestness is ripe.

The Childhood Longing

An illustration: From childhood, there was an inexplicable longing. Not for toys, friends, or success. But for something unnamed, something that all the normal pursuits of life didn't address.

By teenage years, this crystallized into words: "All I desire is moksha. Nothing else will satisfy me."

Not as a spiritual performance. Not as identity. But as a simple fact. The way someone might say "I'm hungry" or "I'm tired." Just stating what is.

Even in ordinary family situations, this showed itself. When relatives asked - as they inevitably do - "When do you want to get married?" the answer was immediate and honest: "I must have done that in many past lives. Why now? It's only moksha now."

Not rudeness. Not rejection of life. But clarity about what actually mattered. Marriage, career, success - perhaps important, perhaps necessary, but not the point. Not what this birth was for.

This wasn't cultivated. Wasn't earned through practices. It was simply there - perhaps from past lives, perhaps grace, perhaps the mysterious workings of consciousness recognizing its own incompleteness in the play of separation.

Years later, my final teacher would say directly: "End this love relationship with your beloved, the god that you think is close to you, whom you devote your time and effort to." This was the ultimate test - letting go even of Sai Baba, even of the devotional relationship that had sustained me since childhood. Even that had to be surrendered. Not because devotion was wrong, but because even the most sacred relationship can become an obstacle when it's used to avoid the final dissolution of the one who relates.

For some, this earnestness is innate. Born with it. The fire burning from the start.

For most people, it develops throughout life. Through suffering. Through the gradual recognition that nothing external ever truly satisfies. Through picking up stone after stone and finding none are gems.

Both paths are valid. Both lead to the same place.

The only question is: Is earnestness present now? Not yesterday, not tomorrow, but now?

When Earnestness Is Absent

Without earnestness, spiritual seeking becomes comfortable.

You read books - interesting philosophy. You attend retreats - nice experiences. You practice meditation - pleasant relaxation. You discuss non-duality - intellectual stimulation.

All valuable perhaps. All pointing in the right direction.

But nothing moves. Nothing dissolves. The seeker remains intact, maybe even strengthened by all the spiritual activity.

Because you're not actually willing to die. Not willing to give up being someone. Not willing to lose your comfortable position as a spiritual seeker, making progress on the path.

Teachers can point. Teachings can be clear. Methods can be direct.

But without earnestness, they bounce off. Or get absorbed into the seeker's collection. Or become part of the spiritual identity.

Nothing fundamental changes because you're not desperate for fundamental change.

You want improvement. Not dissolution. You want better states. Not the end of the experiencer. You want enlightenment as achievement. Not the recognition that there's no one to achieve it.

The Moment Earnestness Ripens

You'll know.

Not because someone tells you. Not because you complete some requirement.

But because you can't continue anymore.

Can't read one more book. Can't try one more practice. Can't attend one more retreat. Can't hope for one more future attainment.

The exhaustion is complete. The seeking has burned itself out. The person is so tired of being a seeker that even that identity must go.

And in that exhaustion, that giving up, that surrender - earnestness is fully present.

Not as something you have. But as what remains when everything else falls away.

When earnestness ripens, a simple question from a teacher cuts through decades of seeking. A single pointer dissolves lifetimes of accumulation. A direct look reveals what was always obvious.

Because there's nothing left to protect. Nothing left to preserve. Nothing left to lose.

Only the desperate need for what's real.

And that need is itself the beginning of the end of seeking.

For You, Measuring Your Earnestness

Don't fool yourself about this.

Don't claim earnestness you don't have. Don't pretend to be more desperate than you are. Don't perform spiritual urgency.

But also, don't assume earnestness must look a certain way.

It's not about drama or intensity or declaring yourself ready. It's about simple, honest assessment:

Right now, this moment - if you had to choose between truth and everything else, what would you choose?

If truth meant losing your comfortable life, your relationships, your identity, your accumulated spiritual knowledge, your hope for future happiness - would you still choose it?

Not "would you theoretically" but actually - would you?

If yes, without hesitation - earnestness is present.

If no, or if there's doubt - that's fine. Keep seeking. Keep living. Let life exhaust the alternatives. Earnestness will ripen when it ripens.

But don't waste time with final teachings before earnestness is present. Don't sit with teachers who demand everything when you're only willing to give something.

Wait. Seek. Exhaust yourself. Pick up stones until you're tired of stones.

And when earnestness finally ripens - when you truly cannot continue seeking one more day - then come.

Then the final teacher can work.

Then the pointing can land.

Then the dissolution can happen.

Not because you earned it.

But because you're finally ready to lose everything.

And in that readiness, everything is already lost.

Only truth remains.

Not because you found it.

But because everything else fell away, and what remains is what was always here.

The Question That Reveals Everything

So ask yourself now, honestly:

How important is this to you?

Really. Not what you think you should say. Not what sounds spiritual.

But actually - how important is truth to you?

If the answer is "very important, but..." - then keep seeking.

If the answer is "nothing else matters" and you mean it with your entire being - then you're ready.

The teaching is simple. The method is direct. The recognition is immediate.

But only if earnestness is present.

Without it, you're just collecting more stones.

With it, the seeking ends.

Not gradually. Not eventually. But now.

Look.

CHAPTER 6: The Investigation

What Self-Enquiry Actually Is

You've heard about self-enquiry. Read Ramana's teachings on "Who am I?" Perhaps even tried it as a practice.

I sat at Ramana's ashram in Tiruvannamalai, asking "Who am I?" repeatedly. Nothing happened. No insight, no breakthrough, no recognition. Why? Because I was seeking deeply. The very intensity of seeking was the obstacle.

Most people misunderstand what self-enquiry actually is.

They think it's a meditation technique. A method to repeat. A question to ask mentally and wait for an answer.

It's none of these things.

Self-enquiry is not a practice. It's an investigation. And there's a profound difference.

Practice vs. Investigation

Practice implies:

- Someone doing something
- Repetition to achieve mastery
- Progress over time
- A goal to reach through effort

Investigation implies:

- Direct looking right now
- No repetition needed
- Nothing to master

- Only seeing what's already here

When you practice self-enquiry, you confirm the practitioner. "I am doing self-enquiry to become enlightened." The person remains intact, even strengthened by spiritual practice.

When you investigate, the investigator is what's being investigated. And when you look for the investigator, you cannot find them. If they are not found, the entire structure collapses.

This is not practice. This is seeing.

The Question "Who Am I?"

Ramana's question seems simple: "Who am I?"

But it's not meant to be answered by the mind. The mind will immediately produce answers:

- "I am this body"
- "I am this mind"
- "I am consciousness"
- "I am the Self"

All of these are thoughts. Concepts. Ideas about what you are.

The question "Who am I?" is intended to redirect attention inward. To look for the one asking. To search for the "I" directly, not conceptually.

It's like asking: "Where is the seeker?"

And when you actually look - not think about it, not philosophize, but actually look - what do you find?

Can you locate this "I"? Can you point to it? Can you prove it exists as anything other than a thought that arises?

How to Actually Investigate

Stop reading for a moment.

Right now, look for yourself.

Not your body - that's an object you perceive. Not your thoughts - those are objects appearing in awareness. Not your feelings - those, too, are perceived.

But YOU - the one perceiving all of this. Where are you?

Don't think about it. Don't imagine an answer. Actually look.

Turn attention back on itself. Try to find the observer—the witness. The "I" that seems to be reading these words.

Where is it?

...

What did you find?

If you're honest, you'll notice: you cannot find yourself as an object. You cannot locate an "I" that exists independently of thoughts about "I."

Thoughts arise: "I am here." "I am the one reading." "I am aware."

But these are just thoughts. Where is the actual "I" they refer to?

Look again. Keep looking. Don't settle for conceptual answers.

This is investigation.

What the Investigation Reveals

When you look for the "I" and cannot find it, one of several things happens:

1. The mind produces more thoughts: "But I must be here, I'm thinking these thoughts!" "I'm the awareness behind the thoughts!" "I'm the body experiencing this!"

These are all thoughts. More concepts. The mind trying to save itself.

Don't believe them. Keep looking. Where is the actual "I" that these thoughts refer to?

2. Frustration arises: "I can't find it. I'm doing something wrong. This isn't working."

Good. The frustration is the seeker realizing it cannot find itself. This frustration is progress, not failure.

3. A gap opens: For a moment, there are no thoughts. Just looking. Just presence. Just awareness without an "I" claiming it.

This gap is the beginning of recognition. Not an experience. Not a state. But the simple seeing: there's awareness, but no one who is aware. There's seeing, but no seer. There's living, but no liver.

4. The mind regroups: After the gap, the mind returns: "I just had an experience! I saw there's no self! I get it now!"

And in that moment, the seeker has reformed. The "I" is back, now claiming to have understood no-self.

This is the trap. Recognizing no-self becomes another experience for someone. Understanding non-duality becomes another achievement.

The investigation must continue. Not just once, but persistently, until even the one who "gets it" is seen through.

The Investigation Is Not Meditation

Meditation often involves:

- Watching the breath
- Observing thoughts
- Resting in awareness
- Cultivating presence

All valuable. All useful as preparation.

But self-enquiry is different. It's not passive watching. It's an active investigation. Hunting for the "I." Refusing to accept conceptual answers. Demanding direct seeing.

It's the difference between:

- Watching clouds pass in the sky (meditation)
- Looking for the sky itself, then realizing you can't find it as an object because you ARE it (investigation)

The investigation is ruthless. It's not for the faint-hearted. It doesn't settle for peace, for presence, for states of no-thought.

It demands: Where is the "I?" Show me. Prove it exists. Point to it.

And when you cannot, when every attempt to locate the self fails, when every concept is seen as just another thought - what remains?

Common Mistakes in Investigation

Mistake 1: Asking the question mentally and waiting for an answer

"Who am I? ... I am pure consciousness."

This is not an investigation. This is mental gymnastics. The mind answering its own question with concepts it already has.

Correct approach: Don't wait for an answer. Look directly. Turn attention on itself. Try to find the one asking.

Mistake 2: Creating a witness position

"I am the witness observing all experiences."

This is subtle, but it's still a position. Still someone claiming to be the witness.

Correct approach: Look for the witness. Where is it? Can you find it? Or is "witness" just another thought?

Mistake 3: Resting in awareness

"I'll just be awareness, rest as awareness, abide in the Self."

Who is resting? Who is abiding? This creates someone who has achieved a state of being awareness.

Correct approach: Is there someone aware? Or just awareness, with no one claiming it?

Mistake 4: Stopping after a glimpse

"I saw there's no self! I had a recognition!"

Who saw? Who had the recognition? The seeker has just found a new identity: "enlightened person who knows there's no self."

Correct approach: Keep investigating. Look for the one who "saw." Look for the one who "knows." Don't stop until even the knower is gone.

When to Investigate

The beautiful thing about self-enquiry: it can be done anytime, anywhere, in any state.

An illustration: After meeting my final teacher, I spent hours, days, months looking in the direction she pointed to. I would book hotel rooms in my own city, pretending to work, but actually doing nothing but this looking. Walking in the room - who's walking? Eating - who's eating? Showering - who's showering? Even during phone arguments, in the middle of anger rising, the looking would cut through: who's arguing?

Trips to the Far East, to India, wherever I went - this looking was of primary importance. Not sightseeing, not spiritual tourism, but relentless looking in the direction pointed. In airports, on trains, in temples - who is traveling? Who is seeking? Where is this one?

Every moment became an opportunity. Not as discipline, but as a desperate need. The question wouldn't leave: Where is this "I" everyone assumes exists?

When peace arises: Who feels peaceful? When disturbance arises: Who is disturbed? When thought appears: Who thinks? When action happens: Who acts?

Look. Don't answer conceptually. Look directly for the one these things are happening to.

An illustration: Once, in the middle of a phone argument, the investigation happened spontaneously. The anger was building, and the sense of "I'm right, they're wrong" was strong. Then suddenly: Who is arguing?

Looking for the arguer. Cannot find them. Just arguing is happening, with no one doing it.

The whole drama collapsed. Not because the anger was suppressed. But because the one who would be angry couldn't be found.

This is the power of investigation. It works in any situation. Because every situation has the same assumption: there's someone to whom this is happening.

Challenge that assumption. Look for that someone. See what's actually true.

The Final Stage: Investigating the Investigator

At some point, the investigation becomes very subtle.

You've seen through the gross identifications: "I am the body," "I am the thoughts."

You've seen through subtle identifications: "I am awareness," "I am the witness."

But there's still one identification left: "I am the one investigating."

This is the final layer—the investigator itself.

Who is investigating? Can you find them?

When you look for the one doing self-enquiry, what happens?

No one there. Just the investigation happening. Self investigating itself. Awareness knowing itself. No separate investigator needed.

This is when self-enquiry is complete. Not because you've finished a practice. But because there's no one left to practice. The seeker has been completely seen through. The investigator has investigated itself out of existence.

What remains is not "you" who are enlightened.

But just this. Just awareness. Just presence. Just what is.

Without anyone claiming it. Without anyone knowing it. Without anyone being it.

Just this.

The Role of the Teacher in Investigation

You can investigate alone. Ramana himself did.

But most people need guidance. Because the mind is subtle. The seeker is clever. The strategies for avoiding the final seeing are infinite.

A teacher sees through your tricks. Points out when you're answering conceptually rather than looking directly. Refuses to let you settle for partial seeing. Pushes you past the point where you would stop and claim understanding.

The teacher doesn't give you the answer. Cannot give you the answer. Because any answer would just be another concept for the seeker to hold.

Instead, the teacher keeps pointing you back to the investigation: Look. Look again. Look more directly. Don't stop looking until there's no one left who's looking.

This is what happened in that month with my final teacher—not being given teachings to understand. But being forced to investigate until every last hiding place of the seeker was exposed.

Not comfortable. Not gentle. But effective.

Because the teacher doesn't care about your comfort. Doesn't care about your spiritual progress. Only cares about whether you're actually seeing or still fooling yourself.

For You, Reading This

Don't just read about self-enquiry. Don't just understand it conceptually.

Investigate now.

Put this book down. Look for yourself. Who is reading? Where are they? Can you find them?

Don't settle for "I am the body reading." Look at the body. It's an object you perceive. You're not it.

Don't settle for "I am the mind reading." Watch thoughts. They come and go. You're aware of them. You're not them.

Don't settle for "I am awareness." Look for awareness as an object. Can you find it? Or is it what's looking, not what's seen?

Keep investigating until the investigator disappears.

Until there's just this.

Reading happening. Awareness present. Life unfolding.

With no one at the center of it claiming ownership.

This is not an achievement to reach.

It's the seeing that there never was anyone to reach anything.

And that seeing is available now.

Not after more practice. Not after more preparation. Not after reading the rest of this book.

But now.

Look.

Who are you?

Can you find yourself?

When you cannot, what remains?

That is the answer.

Not as concept.

As direct seeing.

Investigate.

CHAPTER 7: Truth

The Ultimate Recognition

Whatever one can conceive actually does not exist.

This is the beginning of understanding. Not as philosophy, but as direct seeing.

The moment you think of something - enlightenment, freedom, God, self - that very conception is a boundary around the boundless. The infinite cannot be conceived. It cannot be contained in thought. So whatever your mind grasps, whatever it defines, whatever it names - that is not it.

Yet Truth is not nothing.

It is empty, yes. But full. Overflowing. More present than presence itself. Like space - utterly empty, yet containing everything.

The Illusion of Creation

Every creation, even the tiniest pebble or microorganism, actually does not exist as an independent, separate entity.

This is not nihilism. The pebble appears. The microorganism functions. But in their own right, separated from the whole - they do not truly exist. They appear in what can only be called true synchronicity. Perfect timing, perfect placement, perfect unfoldment.

This synchronicity is so perfect, so seamless, that it creates the magnificent illusion we call "life."

The illusion is so complete that we fall for it utterly. We believe in the pebble's solidity, the microorganism's separateness, the person's autonomy. We believe in causality, in time, in becoming.

All illusion. All appearance. All maya.

When Life Actually Happens

Life actually only happens when everything is lost.

Not philosophically lost. Lived loss. Not an iota of physical or material existence remains. Not a thread of identity. Not a vestige of the one who was seeking, becoming, achieving.

When all is lost - when the seeker gives up completely, when the person dissolves entirely, when every last pretense of being somebody is seen through - then Life happens.

Not "my life" or "your life."

But Life itself. Pure, undirected, uncaused. Happening through this body-mind as it happens through the pebble, through the bird, through the universe itself.

Truth Shining Naked

When all is lost, Truth shines as naked as ever.

Not hidden, not distant, not requiring achievement.

Naked. Obvious. Always here. Always now. The ground on which everything appears.

Like discovering that what you were searching for in distant mountains was beneath your feet all along.

Except it was never beneath your feet. Your feet were in it. You were it. Always.

The Reflection of Reality

What we see in apparent reality is only its reflection.

The world is real, yes - as appearance. As play. As the dance of consciousness.

But it is a reflection, not a source. Shadow, not substance. The finger pointing at the moon, not the moon itself.

The one who seeks the world as ultimate reality is like someone seeking their face in the mirror instead of turning around.

Truth Is Everywhere

Truth is present everywhere, in everything.

Not distributed. Not located. But omnipresent.

In the form that appears as a person, in the thought that arises, in the sensation that is felt, in the space that contains all of this.

There is no place where Truth is not.

And therefore, paradoxically, there is nowhere to go to find it.

What Remains Is Truth Alone

When all concepts dissolve, when all seeking ends, when the seeker is seen as illusion - what remains?

Not "you" remaining. Not an enlightened person abiding in bliss.

But the simple, undeniable fact: Truth remains. Always was. Always will be.

Not as something to attain, but as the only thing that never left.

The Ultimate Summary

As Ramana Maharshi declared in *Self-Realization*:

There is no creation or destruction. No destiny or free will. No path or liberation.

This is the ultimate truth.

Not because Ramana said it, though his words point precisely here.

But because direct seeing reveals exactly this:

The appearance of creation arises in what was never created. The sense of becoming happens in what never changes. The illusion of bondage appears in what was never bound.

The liberation you seek is the recognition that you were never imprisoned.

The path you walk leads nowhere because you are already here.

The freedom you desire is the understanding that there is no one to be free.

And Then?

Life continues—the body functions. Relationships happen. Work occurs. Suffering may appear. Joy may arise. Fear may come. Love may flow.

All of it, in the recognition that none of it is happening to anyone.

All of it, in the knowing that what you are cannot be touched, changed, or affected by any of it.

All of it, as the play of consciousness knowing itself.

Yet even this must be refined: What you are is beyond even consciousness. Beyond awareness. Beyond being.

Consciousness arises and subsides in various states, including waking and sleep. Awareness comes and goes. Even the sense "I Am" appears and disappears.

But what you are never moves. Never changes. Cannot be known or experienced because it is prior to all knowing, all experiencing.

This is Nisargadatta's ultimate pointing: "I am not consciousness. I am that which is aware of consciousness arising."

Not as something to grasp. Not as a higher understanding to achieve. But as the recognition that even the subtlest identification - "I am awareness" - is still a position, still within consciousness, still not what you ultimately are.

What remains when even consciousness is seen as appearance?

That cannot be said. Cannot be known. Cannot be experienced.

It simply is.

Prior to all that appears.

Beyond all that can be conceived.

The absolute reality.

Not as belief. Not as hope. Not as spiritual attainment.

But as the simple, undeniable reality that was always already the case.

CHAPTER 8: The Three Masters Unified

One Truth, Three Doors

Three masters guided my journey. Each pointed differently. Each was perfect for what was needed at that moment. Yet all three pointed to the same recognition: There is nobody. There never was.

Sai Baba - The Biggest Hand

People came to Sai Baba from 1870 until his Mahasamadhi in 1918. Most came for material wealth - money, health, family prosperity, worldly solutions. This was not wrong. This was the beginning.

A few elite and deeply devoted came seeking truth itself. These were rare.

Baba's way of handling all was unique. He would say or do something to one person, but the pointing was meant for another. Only if the person could gather what he actually said, if they took the lesson to heart, did their life change from within.

For many, he sat there and fulfilled their wishes. Why? To slow the mind. To create stillness. To prepare the ground.

When the mind gets what it seeks - health restored, money problems solved, family conflicts resolved - it settles momentarily. In that settling, if one is ready and watching, truth can slip through.

Some were lucky with that recognition. Many could not understand the pointing.

In his every word, deed, and action, Baba directed people to the truth. But people had to be really committed to the search to see it.

The answer was always there, hidden in plain sight. In his enigmatic responses. In his apparent contradictions. In his silence.

Baba's path is the path of the biggest hand.

The hand that holds you when you're not ready to stand alone. The hand that fulfills desires until desire itself is exhausted. The hand that uses devotion - the love between devotee and deity - to gradually dissolve the separation between them.

This is the longest path because it meets you where you are—seeking worldly things? Fine. Baba gives them, until you see they don't satisfy. Seeking spiritual experiences? He gives those too, until you see experiences come and go.

The biggest hand carries you until you're ready for the medium hand.

Ramana Maharshi - The Medium Hand of Inquiry

Ramana went straight to the point.

The place he sat in Arunachala was where people went to get answers for their most important questions. Not worldly questions - these seekers had already exhausted that. They came because nothing else had satisfied.

Ramana was a catalyst. In his presence, the mind froze. Not through force or technique, but through the sheer obviousness of what he was. Silence speaking louder than words.

In that frozen moment, if his pointing was clear and solid, if the seeker was ready, it immediately landed at the ultimate truth.

His method was "Who am I?" - the simplest question with the most devastating answer. Because when you actually look for the "I" that asks the question, you cannot find it. And in not finding it, the seeker dissolves. What remains is what always was.

One instance of this directness was his dialogue with Papaji, the great master who later gave Satsang in Lucknow. Papaji came to Ramana seeking God. Ramana asked him to find out who is seeking God. That single pointing was enough. Papaji recognized himself, and later helped several students realize the same truth. Some of his students continue sharing these teachings today.

Ramana's path is the medium hand. It gives you a method - self-enquiry. Something you can practice, apply, and investigate with. Not gradual in the sense of progressive stages, but direct in its approach. You look now. You look again. You keep looking until the looker dissolves.

This is for those who have been carried by the biggest hand and are now ready for direct investigation. For those who cannot wait any longer. For those willing to look relentlessly - right now.

Nisargadatta Maharaj - The Medium Hand of Negation

Nisargadatta went to the same depth as Ramana, but through a different door.

"What I am is beyond consciousness," he declared.

Not just beyond body and mind. Beyond awareness itself. Beyond the witness. Beyond even the "I Am."

His instruction was ruthless in its simplicity: "Abandon false ideas, that is all. There is no need for true ideas. There are none."

Not replace false beliefs with true ones. Not accumulate spiritual knowledge. But drop all concepts - both false and true. Because even the truest idea is still just a thought. Still within consciousness. Still not what you are.

Nisargadatta's path is also the medium hand. It gives you a method - neti-neti, negation. "Not this, not this." You systematically negate every identification until nothing remains to negate. Until even the one negating is seen as an illusion.

This is the most uncompromising of the medium hands. No comfort. No consolation. No building up of spiritual self. Only the stripping away of every last identification until what remains cannot be named, cannot be known, cannot even be said to exist - because it is prior to existence itself.

This is for those who have accumulated spiritual experiences and realized they're still in the mind. For those who know that any state, any attainment, any "I am this" is still bondage. For those ready to negate everything, including the negator.

The Synthesis - Three Hands, One Truth

My teacher put it perfectly, though I now see it more clearly:

There are three hands leading to truth:

The biggest hand - for you to get closer to the truth through devotion and grace.

The medium hand - to show you the method of direct inquiry and negation.

The smallest hand - to help you realize it completely, or rather, to be found by it.

The Biggest Hand - Sai Baba

Sai Baba's way - holds you, carries you, prepares you gradually over lifetimes if needed. It meets you in your worldliness, your desires, your devotion. It doesn't reject where you are. It works with it, through it, until you're ready for something more direct.

This hand is infinitely patient. It fulfills wishes, grants experiences, builds devotion - all to exhaust the seeker's strategies. All to create the earnestness needed for the direct path.

This is where most seekers begin. This is the grace that prepares the ground.

The Medium Hand - Ramana and Nisargadatta

Ramana and Nisargadatta's way - gives you the method. Shows you how to investigate. Teaches you to ask "Who am I?" or to negate "not this, not this."

These are still teachings you can practice. Still, there are methods you can apply. Still, there are paths you can follow.

But they're direct. They cut through the gradually accumulated spiritual knowledge and point you to immediate investigation.

Ramana gives self-enquiry. Nisargadatta gives ruthless negation. Both are methods that, when applied earnestly, dissolve the seeker.

But there's still someone practicing the method. Still someone doing self-enquiry. Still someone negating.

This is necessary. This is the refinement. But it's not yet the final step.

The Smallest Hand - The Final Teacher

The smallest hand - Dolano, Namkei, and those like them - doesn't give you methods. Doesn't give you practices. Doesn't give you anything to do.

The smallest hand points and says: "Stop. Look now. Not later. Not through practice. Now. Where is the one who would practice?"

This pointing is final because it leaves absolutely no room for seeking. No path to follow. No practice to do. No gradual improvement. No future attainment.

Just: Look here. See this. There is nothing to become. There is no one becoming it. Stop everything and recognize what's already obvious.

This is surgical. Immediate. Uncompromising.

The smallest hand doesn't hold you. Doesn't guide you step by step. It simply points to what's here, and if you're ready - if the biggest hand has prepared you, if the medium hand has taught you how to look - then recognition is immediate.

Not as an achievement. But as seeing what was always already the case.

Which Hand Do You Need?

If you are still deeply identified with being a person, with worldly desires, with the need for security and comfort - **Sai Baba's path** of devotion and surrender is where you start. Let the biggest hand hold you. Let grace work through desire until desire exhausts itself. This may take lifetimes. But it's a necessary preparation.

If you have exhausted worldly seeking, had glimpses, know intellectually that you are not the body-mind but need a method to investigate directly - **Ramana's self-enquiry or Nisargadatta's negation** is your door. These are the medium hands. They give you the tools: "Who am I?" or "Not this, not this." Apply these relentlessly until the questioner dissolves.

If you have done the practices, applied the methods, investigated earnestly, and are exhausted with even spiritual seeking itself - you're ready for **the smallest hand**. The final teacher who gives you nothing to do, no path to follow, but simply points: Look now. There is nobody. There never was. Stop and see.

But here is the ultimate truth:

All three hands lead to the same recognition.

That there is no person. That there never was a separate self. That what you are cannot be found because it is not an object. That what you are cannot be lost because it was never separate.

The recognition is identical whether you arrive through devotion, inquiry, or negation, or through the final pointing.

Sai Baba, Ramana, Nisargadatta, and the final teachers - all expressions of one consciousness, offering different hands to different seekers at different stages, all pointing to the same home.

The home that was never left. The truth that was always obvious. The self that is not self. The nobody that is everything.

In My Journey

In my journey, I needed all three hands.

Sai Baba's biggest hand held me from childhood, through decades of seeking, through the surgery and prayer at Ganeshpuri. His grace prepared the ground, exhausted my worldly seeking, and created the earnestness that would not be satisfied with anything less than truth.

Ramana's medium hand gave me the method. Six years of Zen practice with Fr. Ama Samy, sitting with koans, learning to investigate "Who am I?" The recognition by the rivulet in Kodaikanal - all echoes of Ramana's direct pointing. This taught me how to look.

Nisargadatta's medium hand refined the looking. His ruthless "beyond consciousness," his "abandon all ideas," his neti-neti - this showed me that even awareness is appearance, even the witness must be witnessed.

The smallest hand - Dolano and Namkei - gave the final push. No more methods. No more practices. Just Stop. Look now. There is nobody. The three months with Namkei clearing away clouds. The month with Dolano dismantling every last defense. The pointing that left no escape, no spiritual position to cling to, no seeker to reform.

All three hands were necessary. All were one movement of grace.

And you, reading this, are the same one consciousness that expressed as Baba's devotion, as Ramana's inquiry, as Nisargadatta's negation, as Dolano's final pointing.

The same one that writes these words. The same one that seeks and finds itself. The same one playing all roles in this cosmic dance.

Which hand do you need now?

Look and see.

CHAPTER 9: For The Reader

Direct Transmission

My humble salutations to each one of you.

Which is actually me, but I appear different.

This is not poetic. This is direct seeing. The one reading these words - that is me. The one who wrote them - that is you. There is only one consciousness, appearing as many, seeking itself through infinite forms.

This recognition changes nothing and changes everything.

This Birth Is For Recognition

This birth is for you to realize the ultimate truth.

Not to accumulate, not to achieve, not to become better or more spiritual.

But to recognize what you already are.

That's it. That's the only point of this appearance.

Everything else—career, relationships, success, failure, experiences, states—all secondary. All permitted, but none essential. None the point.

The point is one thing only: The recognition of Truth.

And then see how things unfold.

Everything Changes, Nothing Changes

Every apparent reality remains the same.

The world doesn't disappear. Your body doesn't vanish. People are still people. Work is still work. Pain still hurts. Joy still delights.

The pebble is still a pebble. The bird still sings. The sun still rises and sets.

Nothing in the apparent reality changes.

But everything has changed.

Your way of looking at things becomes different.

Not that you develop a new philosophy or adopt a better perspective.

But the one doing the looking is seen through as an illusion.

What remains is just looking. Just seeing. Without a seer claiming it.

Your way of looking at yourself becomes different.

No longer seeking to improve, fix, perfect this "me."

But seeing that the "me" was never real to begin with.

Your perspective on everything else changes.

Because when you see through yourself, you see through the illusion of separateness everywhere.

The other is you. The world is you. God is you. Even the one you thought you were is you.

The Play Becomes Fuller

You enjoy this play more fully.

Not because you become more spiritual or transcend the world.

But because there's no one resisting it anymore.

No one is clinging to it.

No one is pushing it away.

Just the play happening, completely, without obstruction.

And in that completeness, there's a joy that has nothing to do with circumstances.

Why You Come and Leave With Nothing

And then you realize the truth as to why you come and leave without anything of this world.

The ultimate irony.

You came with nothing. You leave with nothing. In between, you accumulate, cling, worry, and protect.

But why do you leave with nothing?

Because nothing was ever yours to begin with.

Because you are not the person who owns things.

Because what you are cannot accumulate or lose anything.

Because when nothing really exists, how can it bring or take anything?

This is the final understanding.

The world appears. Life happens. Experiences arise. But in their own right, independently, as solid separate entities - they do not truly exist.

So how can they take anything from you? How can they give you anything?

They can only appear to do so.

And in that appearance, there is freedom.

The freedom of one who knows: *Nothing can actually be gained or lost because there is no one to gain or lose it.*

If You Are Still Seeking

So if you are still seeking, still practicing, still hoping to become enlightened:

Look directly at who is seeking.

Look directly at who practices.

Look directly at who hopes.

Can you find them? Can you point to them? Can you prove they exist?

When you look and cannot find the seeker, what remains?

That is the truth.

Not an experience to seek. Not a state to achieve. Not something future.

But the simple, obvious, undeniable reality of what you are right now.

Before any seeking began. After all, seeking ends. Whether seeking happens or not.

This is what this book points to.

This is what every master points to.

This is what your own direct seeing will reveal.

If you are ready.

If you are earnest.

If you stop postponing and look now.

Final Salutation

My salutations to you, which is me, which is all of us, which is the one consciousness knowing itself through infinite appearances.

May the seeking end.

May the seeker be seen.

May the truth that you are be obvious.

May this birth, this appearance, serve that alone.

CHAPTER 10: There Is Nobody

The Final Step

You've read the book. You understand intellectually. You've had glimpses. You know the teachings.

Now what?

Stop reading about it. Stop understanding it. Stop waiting for the right moment.

Look now.

Not tomorrow. Not after one more practice. Not when you feel more ready.

Now.

What Actually Changes

After recognition, life looks ordinary. Completely ordinary.

The body wakes up. Thoughts arise. Actions happen. The world appears.

However, there's no one at the center claiming it. Nobody is making it serious. Nobody is turning it into "my life" with "my problems."

Work happens - without stress about outcomes. Relationships continue - without neediness or defense. Pain arises - without suffering. Joy appears - without grasping.

Everything is the same. Everything different.

Not because you've achieved a special state. But because the one who would achieve anything was never real.

The Final Instruction

My teacher's last practical pointer: There are passive thoughts and active thoughts.

Passive thoughts drift through like the weather. Let them.

Active thoughts create a thinker. They assert, "I need to figure this out," "I should have done differently," "What if..."

When active thoughts arise: **Shut up.**

Simple. Clear. Direct.

Not violently. Just firmly cutting through before the thought can create a person who thinks it.

And here is the complete teaching, the essence of everything:

A silent mind is the source. An active source is the mind.

That's all there is.

Nothing more. Nothing less. The entire teaching in two sentences.

When the mind is silent - when active thoughts aren't creating a thinker - what remains is source. Pure being. Consciousness itself. No person. No seeker. No one separate from what is.

When the source becomes active - when it moves, when it thinks, when it creates the sense of "I" - that activity IS the mind. The source appears as a person. The infinite appearing as finite. The one appearing as many.

But it's always just source. Always just consciousness. Sometimes silent, sometimes active. Sometimes resting in itself, sometimes moving as mind and world and person.

This movement - from silence to activity, from source to mind, from being to becoming - this IS life. This IS the play. This IS all there is.

You cannot stop this movement. Cannot maintain permanent silence. Cannot keep the mind from becoming active again.

But you can see it. See the mechanism. See how the person is created moment by moment through active thought.

And in that seeing, identification breaks. Not permanently - the person may reform. But each time it's seen, it's seen as an illusion. As appearance. As a source playing at being someone.

Eventually, the seeing becomes natural. Automatic. The person still appears when needed - for functioning, for relating, for living. But there's no belief in it anymore. No identification with it. No taking it seriously.

Just source, sometimes silent, sometimes active. Sometimes nobody, sometimes somebody. Always just this. Always complete. Always free.

That's all there is.

Nothing to achieve beyond seeing this clearly. Nothing to become beyond recognizing what already is.

The search ends not because you found something. But because you saw there's only one source, playing all roles, pretending to seek itself, then recognizing itself again.

Simple. Obvious. Complete.

Beyond Consciousness - Nisargadatta's Ultimate Pointing

Most spiritual teachings stop at recognizing yourself as awareness, as consciousness, as the witness. "I am not the body-mind, I am pure awareness." This is a significant recognition. It dissolves identification with the person.

But Nisargadatta went further. Much further.

He insisted: "What I am is beyond consciousness itself."

This sounds paradoxical. How can you be beyond awareness when awareness is all there is?

But Nisargadatta was pointing to something radical: Consciousness itself arises. It appears in waking, subsides in deep sleep, and returns again. Even the sense "I Am" comes and goes—states of awareness change. Experiences of consciousness vary.

So if consciousness itself appears and disappears, what is it appearing IN? What is aware of consciousness arising?

That - that which is prior to consciousness, prior to awareness, prior to even the sense of being - that is what you are.

Not as something to experience. You cannot experience what you are because experience itself happens within consciousness. You cannot be conscious of what is prior to consciousness.

This is not nihilism. Not nothingness in the sense of void or absence.

It is the absolute reality - prior to existence and non-existence both. Prior to manifestation. Prior to the very sense "I Am."

Nisargadatta called it the Absolute. The Parabrahman. But even these are just pointers to what cannot be named, cannot be known, cannot be experienced.

Why does this matter?

Because even the position "I am awareness" is still a position. Still a subtle identification. Still something the mind can cling to—still a "me" who is aware.

When even consciousness is seen as appearance - when even the witness is witnessed - what remains is utterly beyond all positions, all identities, all concepts.

This is the final dissolution. Not of consciousness, but of any identification with consciousness.

You are not awareness having experiences. You are not consciousness manifesting as form. You are not even being itself.

You are that which all of this appears in - prior to it, beyond it, untouched by whether it appears or not.

This cannot be grasped. Cannot be understood. Cannot be experienced.

It can only be recognized as what was always already the case - before seeking began, before consciousness arose, before existence itself.

Nothing Is Even Happening

Right now, whatever you think is happening - work pressure, relationship drama, health concerns, spiritual seeking - is not actually happening.

Not as denial. As direct seeing.

There's appearance. Vivid, complete appearance. But there's no one to whom it's appearing. No one for whom it's real. No one who needs to manage, control or fix it.

The dream appears. But you were never in the dream. You are that in which the dream appears.

Even calling it "you" is too much. There is no you. There never was.

Just this. Appearing. Without anyone experiencing it.

How the Search Actually Ends

Not with a bang. Not with cosmic experience. Not with permanent bliss or supernatural powers.

The search ends simply: You look for the seeker and cannot find them.

That's it.

Not "I had an awakening and now I'm enlightened." That's still someone claiming something.

But the direct seeing: There is nobody here. There never was. The entire search was based on a fiction.

What happens after this seeing?

Life continues exactly as before - body wakes, thoughts arise, actions happen. But there's no one at the center making it "my life." No one taking credit or blame. No one hoping it gets better or fearing it gets worse.

Problems may still appear - but there's no problem-haver. Pain may arise - but there's no sufferer. Joy may come - but there's no enjoyer.

Just life, living itself. Consciousness, knowing itself. Existence, unfolding without anyone existing.

Does doubt return? Sometimes. The mind may create the thought, "But am I really free? Shouldn't I feel different?"

These thoughts are seen as thoughts. They're not believed. Or if they are briefly believed, it's quickly seen: "Oh, that's just the mind trying to create a problem again."

The search doesn't end because you reached a permanent state where seeking is impossible. It ends because seeking is seen as pointless - like searching for darkness with a flashlight. The seeker seeking the Self is the Self pretending not to be itself.

When this is obvious, seeking simply stops. Not through effort. Through seeing.

And what remains is not "you enlightened."

What remains is this: ordinary life, without the extraordinary burden of being someone living it.

Simple. Complete. Free.

The End Is The Beginning

When the seeker ends, life begins.

Not "your" life. Just life. Pure. Uncomplicated. Ordinary.

The body functions. Intelligence operates. Love flows. Compassion arises.

But there's no one doing any of it. No one is being spiritual. No one is maintaining enlightenment. No one worried about losing it.

Because there's no one at all.

And in that absence of someone, everything is possible. Everything is complete. Everything is exactly as it should be.

Not because it's perfect. But because there's nobody judging it as imperfect.

Just this.

Always this.

Only this.

The Final Jump

You've come this far. Read all the teachings. Had glimpses. Done practices. Met teachers.

You know intellectually there's nobody. You've even experienced moments where the person dissolved.

But something still seeks. Something still hopes. Something still believes "I need to get this permanently."

That something is the last vestige of the seeker. The subtlest identification. The final claim to being someone.

This must be seen through. Not gradually. Not eventually. Now.

Who is reading these words? Look directly - not at thoughts about "who," but actually look for the reader.

Can you find them? Point to them. Prove they exist as anything other than a thought arising.

When you cannot find them - and you cannot - don't settle for the concept "there's no self." Don't make it another understanding.

Actually see: There is nobody here. Never was. Reading is happening, but there's no reader. Seeking happened, but there was no seeker. Understanding arises, but there's no understander.

This is the jump. Not a movement from here to there. But the seeing that there was never anyone to jump. The cliff was imaginary. The seeker standing on it was fiction.

What remains when this is seen completely?

Life. Simple. Ordinary. Without center. Without owner. Without the burden of being someone.

This is freedom. Not as achievement. As recognition of what was always already the case.

Now

Stop reading.

Put the book down.

Look.

Who are you?

Can you find yourself?

When you cannot, what remains?

Don't think about the answer.

Don't wait for the right moment.

Don't prepare yourself one more time.

Just look.

Now.

The seeking ends here. Not because you found what you sought. But because the seeker was never real.

There is nobody.

There never was.

And this recognition - not as understanding, but as direct seeing - is liberation itself.

Not for someone. Just liberation. Freedom. Truth.

Obvious. Simple. Complete.

Right here. Right now.

Look.

Om Sai Ram

The teaching is complete. The transmission is offered. The rest is up to nobody.

EPILOGUE

For You, The Reader

If this book has pointed you to something true, if the recognition is present even as a glimpse, then understand this:

Don't read this casually. A casual read will do nothing. The mind needs repeated exposure to essential truth. Reread this book. And again. Listen to the teachings repeatedly. Spend time alone with these pointers. Only through this repetition does the mind begin to understand its true nature, to see through its own mechanisms, to exhaust its strategies.

Sit with the truth in solitude. Not in groups discussing concepts. But alone, reading the essential pointers over and over, letting them penetrate deeper each time. The mind is stubborn. It needs persistent, repeated pointing before it surrenders.

When challenges arise - and they will - do instant recognition. In the middle of the storm, when fear grips, anger rises, or pain overwhelms, stop. Look. Who is this happening to? Don't wait for calm. Investigate during the chaos. This is when recognition does its real work.

Each time you recognize difficulty, the situation loses its hold. The grip weakens. The reality of the problem becomes questionable. And slowly - not immediately, but through repeated seeing - you realize: there is no one to whom the situation appears. The situation arises for nobody. And actually, it's not even happening. Not as a solid, substantial reality requiring a response from a person. Just appearance. Just movement in consciousness. Without anyone at the center experiencing it.

Stop collecting teachings. This is the last book you need to read about non-duality. Reading more will only strengthen the seeker.

Stop seeking teachers. If you need guidance, the final teacher will appear when you're ready. But don't make seeking teachers into another spiritual practice.

Look directly. Right now. Not after finishing this page. Who is reading? Can you find them?

Be earnest. If recognition hasn't happened, don't pretend it has. But don't postpone looking either. The urgency is now.

Investigate relentlessly. Every moment. Every situation. Who is experiencing this? Where is the "I"? Don't settle for conceptual answers.

Don't turn this into another identity. "I'm someone who knows there's nobody" is just the seeker in new clothes.

Live it. Not as practice. But as simple seeing: there's functioning without a functioner, living without a liver, experiencing without an experiencer.

If doubt arises: Look again. The doubter is also just a thought. Who doubts? Can you find them?

If you feel lost: Good. The one who would be found was never real. What remains when you're completely lost?

Contact the final teacher if needed: www.friendsofdolano.com - but only if you're truly ready to lose everything.

Otherwise: Close the book. Look. See. Be nobody.

That's all there is.

ACKNOWLEDGMENTS

My deepest gratitude to all the Masters and all who showed the way:

Sri Shirdi Sai Baba - whose grace carried me from childhood, whose love prepared the ground, whose presence remains ever-present.

Sri Ramana Maharshi - whose self-enquiry became the sword that cut through all seeking.

Sri Nisargadatta Maharaj - whose ruthless pointing left no escape, no position to cling to.

Swami Nityananda of Ganeshpuri - at whose samadhi prayers were offered in moments of crisis.

Swami Bhoomananda Tirtha - Whose teachings contributed to the journey.

Dr. Pradeep Ullal – Kundalini Master, whose guidance was invaluable.

Fr. Ama Samy - Zen Master at Perumalmalai Kodaikanal (T.N., India), who introduced the discipline of sitting, the rigor of koans, and six years of patient pointing.

Ramudu - Dear friend, whose Friday morning call opened the door to the final teacher. Without that call, this recognition might have taken many more lifetimes.

Namkei – Deepest gratitude to him as he is the one who spoke truth from wholeness, whose twenty minutes at the cafe revealed that something different was possible, who prepared the ground for what was to come.

Dolano (www.friendsofdolano.com) - The final teacher, who dismantled every defense, exposed every strategy, and pointed relentlessly until there was nobody left—the one who pushed from the cliff.

Papaji (H.W.L. Poonja) - Whose Satsang videos carried the transmission across time and space.

A few friends who helped in many ways, they themselves don't know – Deepa Kishore, Rajesh Nair, Alok Chaubasia, Sandeep Sharma, Sudeep Miranda, Faiza Pacino, and Mahesh Nathani.

Veer and Simba – My lovely pet Chow Chows for lessons learnt from them.

Publishing – Assistance provided by Emily Lisa (USA) for proof reading, Mohamed Rahim (Egypt) for the book cover design and Kamlesh (Pro-Fiverr) for assistance in many ways.

And to all seekers reading this - may the recognition be immediate, the dissolution complete, and the freedom obvious.

There is nobody to thank. There is nobody to be thanked. Yet gratitude flows.

Om Shanti, Let there be peace.

REFERENCES AND BIBLIOGRAPHY

Primary Sources:

- Sri Shirdi Sai Baba - *Sai Satcharita* (Shri Sai Baba Sansthan, Shirdi)
- Ramana Maharshi. *Self-Realization: The Life and Teachings of Ramana Maharshi*. Sri Ramanasramam.
- Nisargadatta Maharaj. *I Am That: Talks with Sri Nisargadatta Maharaj*. Translated by Maurice Frydman. Acorn Press.
- Patanjali. *Yoga Sutras of Patanjali*.

Video/Audio Sources:

- Papaji (H.W.L. Poonja). Satsang videos (various, publicly available online).

Teachers and Masters Acknowledged:

- Swami Nityananda of Ganeshpuri
- Swami Bhoomananda Tirtha (https://www.Narayanatapovanam.com)
- Dr. Pradeep Ullal (https://www.Kevalafoundation.org)
- Fr. Ama Samy - Zen Master (https://www.kanzeonzendo.in)
- Dolano – (https://www.friendsofdolano.com)
- Osho (Bhagwan Shree Rajneesh) - Referenced for teachings (various, publicly available online).
- Joey Lott (https://joeylott.com)
- Naho Owada (https://www.nahoowada.com)
- Tony Parsons (https://www.tonyparsons.com)

Note: While many teachers and masters influenced this journey, direct quotations in the text are cited from *Self-Realization*, *I Am That*, and Papaji's Satsang videos.

About the Author

About the Author

Manoj Kandhari has been on the spiritual path since childhood, held by Sai Baba's grace, refined through Ramana's self-enquiry and Nisargadatta's negation, and trained for six years in Zen practice under Fr. Ama Samy.

Friends in spiritual circles know him as Krishna Chaitanya - a name pointing to pure consciousness (given at Osho Ashram). But names point to nobody.

After decades of seeking, one recognition became clear: as long as you believe you are a person, recognition is impossible. The mind must stop to see this. Just as the book's cover shows - partly crumpled (mind) and partly plain (source) - they are not two. The crumpled is the plain, appearing to be active. The plain is always here, whether mind is active or silent.

When the mind stopped, what remained was obvious: there is nobody here. There never was.

From this seeing, satsangs occur occasionally for those earnest enough to stop seeking and look directly.

This is his first book - though there is nobody writing and nobody reading. Just words appearing as transmission for those standing at the edge.

9 789354 696237

Printed at Repro India Ltd.